Angular Generative AI

Building an intelligent CV enhancer with Google Gemini

Abdelfattah Ragab

Angular Generative AI

Building an intelligent CV enhancer with Google Gemini

Abdelfattah Ragab

Introduction

Welcome to the book "Angular Generative AI: Building an intelligent CV enhancer with Google Gemini".
In this book, I explain how to build an intelligent CV enhancer with Google Gemini.
You will learn how to send prompts to Google Gemini and get answers to your questions.
You will learn how to upload files to the Google AI file manager and attach those files to your prompts.
We will start from scratch and build everything together.
By the end of this book, you will be able to use generative AI in your Angular application and tackle all kinds of scenarios.
Let us get started.

What is Generative AI?

Generative AI refers to a branch of artificial intelligence that focuses on creating new content based on existing data. This technology uses deep learning models to generate high-quality results that can include text, images, audio and even code.

What is Google Gemini?

Google Gemini is an advanced AI model developed by Google to boost creativity and productivity through its chatbot and large language model (LLM) capabilities. It offers users assistance with various tasks, including writing, planning and learning.

Get a Gemini API key

Visit Google AI for Developers and get a Gemini API key

Preview

The application allows users to upload their CV to Gemini and receive feedback on what improvements they should make to be attractive to potential employers.

Enhance your CV

Choose   Send

Enhance your CV

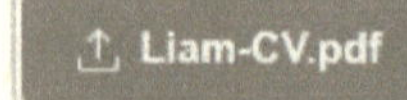

Send

Enhance your CV

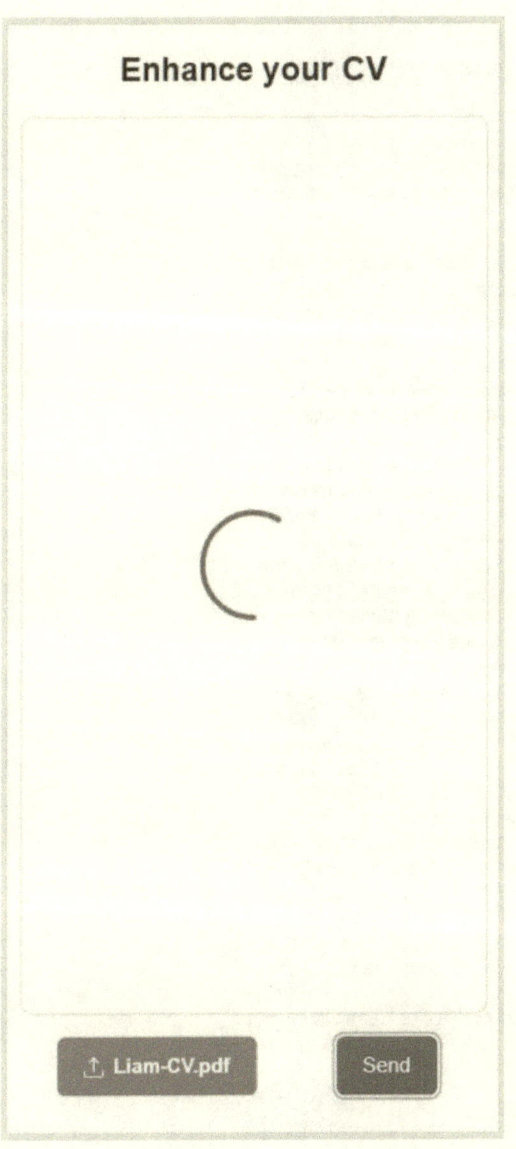

Enhance your CV

Here are some improvements you can make to your CV to make it more appealing to potential employers:

- **Quantify your achievements:** Instead of simply stating that you maintained a high picking/packing speed, provide specific numbers. For example, you could say "Consistently maintained picking/packing speeds in the 98th percentile, exceeding the company average by 10%."
- **Use action verbs:** Use strong action verbs to describe your responsibilities and accomplishments. For example, instead of saying "Performed all warehouse laborer duties," you could say "Managed all aspects of warehouse operations, including packing, picking, counting, record keeping, and maintaining a clean area."
- **Highlight your skills:** Make sure to include a section highlighting your relevant skills, such as inventory management, warehouse sanitation, and operating heavy machinery.
- **Use keywords:** Research common keywords used in job descriptions for the positions you are interested in and incorporate them into your CV.
- **Tailor your CV:** When applying for a specific job, tailor your CV to match the requirements listed in the job description.
- **Proofread carefully:** Before submitting your CV, make sure to proofread it

Choose   Send

Create the Backend

I will create a Nestjs application that will be our backend.
It will be responsible for connecting to the Gemini
server.

```
nest new resume-be
```

Open the project folder in Visual Studio Code.

Use your API key

Create a new **.env** file and add a new entry for the api
key as follows

```
GEMINI_API_KEY=AIz...
```

Install Dependencies

```
npm install @google/generative-ai
@types/multer dotenv
```

This is just one line. We installed
`@google/generative-ai` for the gemini sdk. We
also installed `@types/multer` for uploading files and
`dotenv` for reading the configuration from the **.env** file.

Enable CORS

Enable cors by adding to the **main.ts**

```
app.enableCors();
```

```
  await app.listen(3000);
...
```

Disable .eslintrc.js

Go to the .eslintrc.js file and delete everything inside the
object. Make it an empty object as follows:

```
module.exports = {};
```

Create a new module

```
nest generate module gemini
```

Create a new controller

```
nest generate controller gemini
```

Create a new service

```
nest generate service gemini
```

Gemini Service

First we need to import `GoogleGenerativeAI`,
`GoogleAIFileManager`, `fs` **and** `config`.

```
import { GoogleGenerativeAI } from
'@google/generative-ai';
```

```
import { GoogleAIFileManager } from
'@google/generative-ai/server';
import { Injectable } from
'@nestjs/common';
import * as fs from 'node:fs/promises';

import { config } from 'dotenv';
config();
```

Now I will read the apiKey and save it into a constant
```
const apiKey =
`${process.env.GEMINI_API_KEY}`;
```

In the `GeminiService` **I will declare three private variables**:
```
private genAI;
private model;
private fileManager;
```

I will then initialize it in the constructor
```
constructor() {
  this.genAI = new
GoogleGenerativeAI(process.env.GEMINI_AP
I_KEY);
  this.model =
this.genAI.getGenerativeModel({ model:
'gemini-1.5-flash' });
  this.fileManager = new
GoogleAIFileManager(process.env.GEMINI_A
PI_KEY);
}
```

We set the model to `'gemini-1.5-flash'`

enhanceCV method

I will create a method `enhanceCV` that takes the CV file as a parameter. We will then send this file later from the frontend application.

Upload File to Gemini

To be able to attach the file to the prompt, you must first upload it to the Gemini server.
Gemini provides you with the GoogleAIFileManager, which you can use to upload files. The first parameter is the file path, followed by the mimeType and displayName.
We store all Cvs we receive from the Angular application in the "uploads" folder. We can easily use any file in the uploads folder. After we have finished analyzing the CV and sent the results to the user, we delete all CV files from the Google Manager and from the uploads folder.

```
const uploadResponse = await
this.fileManager.uploadFile(file.path, {
  mimeType: 'application/pdf',
  displayName: file.name,
});
```

Generate Content

We are ready to generate content
```
const result = await
this.model.generateContent([
  {
    fileData: {
      mimeType:
uploadResponse.file.mimeType,
      fileUri: uploadResponse.file.uri,
    },
  },
  'What improvements can I make to this
CV to be of interest to potential
employers?',
]);
```


The `generateContent` **method requires two parameters. The first is the file, the second is the prompt.**
I have set the prompt to the value
```
'What improvements can I make to this
resume to be of interest to potential
employers?'
```
I always send this as a prompt with all resume files.

Now we can return the result, but I have to delete the files first
```
await
this.fileManager.deleteFile(uploadRespon
se.file.name);
```

```
await fs.rm(file.path);
return result.response.text();
```

Our service is ready!

Gemini Controller

Inject the `GeminiService` in the `constructor`

```
constructor(private geminiService:
GeminiService) {}
```

I will create a post endpoint that receives the file from the frontend and calls the Gemini service.
Add the post decorator since it is of type post

```
@Post()
```

We will use interceptors, specifically the file interceptor.

```
@UseInterceptors(
  FileInterceptor('file', {
    storage: diskStorage({
      destination: './uploads',
      filename: (req, file, cb) => {
        const uniqueSuffix =
          Date.now() + '-' +
Math.round(Math.random() * 1e9);
        cb(
          null,
          file.fieldname + '-' +
uniqueSuffix +
extname(file.originalname),
        );
      },
```

```
        }),
    }),
)
```

I configure it so that it saves the files in the **'uploads'** folder and generates a unique name for the files.
Now let's create the method

```
enhanceCV(@UploadedFile() file:
Express.Multer.File) {
    return
this.geminiService.enhanceCV(file);
}
```

It passes the file to the service and returns the result to the frontend.

Debug Enabled

In the Nest application, you can start debugging by clicking on the menu "Run" " → "Start debugging". This works because I added a **launch.json** file in the **.vscode** folder. It contains the configuration for debugging NestJS. Simply add this file to the **.vscode** folder of one of your NestJS applications to enable debugging.

Create the Frontend

```
ng new resume-fe
```
Open the project folder in the Visual Studio Code.

Generate `environments`

```
ng generate environments
```
Add the apiUrl to the environment object as follows
```
export const environment = {
  apiUrl:
'http://localhost:3000/gemini',
};
```

Install Dependencies

```
npm install ngx-markdown marked primeng
```
We use `ngx-markdown` and `marked` to display the
markdown response returned by Gemini.
I use `primeng` components for buttons and file upload.

App Config

Provide both http client and markdown in the
app.config.ts as follows
```
provideHttpClient(withFetch()),
provideMarkdown(),
```

Create a new Service

```
ng g s services/gemini
```

Inject the `HttpClient` in the GeminiService constructor

```
constructor(private http: HttpClient) {}
```

Declare a new method enhanceCV that takes the file as a parameter and call the endpoint

```
enhanceCV(file: any) {
  const formData = new FormData();
  formData.append('file', file);
  return
this.http.post(environment.apiUrl,
formData, {
    responseType: 'text',
  });
}
```

Make sure to set the `responseType` to 'text'

Create a new page

```
ng g c pages/enhance-cv
```

Add it to the routes. Go to **app.routes.ts** and add two new entries, one for the default route and one for our main page

```
{ path: '', redirectTo: 'enhance-cv',
pathMatch: 'full' },
{
  path: 'enhance-cv',
  component: EnhanceCvComponent,
  title: 'Enhance CV - Gemini',
},
```

It is good practice to add titles to all your pages. We will use the `MarkdownComponent`, `ButtonModule`, `FileUploadModule` and `ProgressSpinnerModule` modules. So let's import them first. We will also use the `first()` operator and inject the `GeminiService`. Here are all the component imports:

```typescript
import { Component } from
'@angular/core';
import { MarkdownComponent } from
'ngx-markdown';
import { ButtonModule } from
'primeng/button';
import { FileUploadModule } from
'primeng/fileupload';
import { ProgressSpinnerModule } from
'primeng/progressspinner';
import { first } from 'rxjs';
import { GeminiService } from
'../../services/gemini.service';
```

Make sure to add these modules to the imports array:

```typescript
MarkdownComponent,
ButtonModule,
FileUploadModule,
ProgressSpinnerModule,
```

Declare the following properties inside the component

```typescript
selectedFile: File | null = null;
fileUploadCtrl: any;
answer: any;
```

```
loading = false;
```
Inject the `GeminiService` **in the** `constructor`
```
constructor(private geminiService:
GeminiService) {}
```

onSelectFile

Declare a new method `onSelectFile` with two
parameters; the first is passed from the control and
contains the array files and the second is the reference
to the control for the file upload
```
onSelectFile(e: any, fileUpload: any) {
   this.selectedFile = e.files[0];
   this.fileUploadCtrl = fileUpload;
}
```
It will be called when the user selects the CV file to be
uploaded.

onSend

This method is called when the user clicks on the "Send"
button.
First I check if a CV file is selected, and if so, I set
loading to true and call the Gemini service.
If I get the response, I set the load to false and display
the results.
```
onSend() {
   if (this.selectedFile) {
      this.loading = true;
      this.geminiService
```

```typescript
      .enhanceCV(this.selectedFile)
      .pipe(first())
      .subscribe({
        next: (answer: any) => {
          this.selectedFile = null;
          this.fileUploadCtrl.clear();
          this.answer = answer;
          this.loading = false;
        },
        error: (e) => {
          this.loading = false;
        },
      });
    }
}
```

Now we are done with the component class! So let's move on to the template.

Component Template

First I put a wrapper around everything and create a header

```html
<div class="container">
  <header class="header">Enhance your CV</header>
...
</div>
```

Next, I have to display one of these elements depending on the status of the application: it is loading, or there are already results on the screen, or the user has not yet started the application.

```
@if (loading) {
<p-progressSpinner class="loading"
ariaLabel="loading" />
} @else if(answer) {
<markdown class="answer"
[data]="answer"></markdown>
} @else {
<img class="img-empty" src="empty.jpg"
/>
}
```

Finally, we have the prompt element, which consists of two components: the control for the file upload and the control for the "Send" button.

```
<div class="prompt">
  <p-fileUpload
    mode="basic"
    chooseLabel="Choose"
    chooseIcon="pi pi-upload"
    class="upload"
    (onSelect)="onSelectFile($event,
fileUpload)"
    #fileUpload
  />
  <p-button
(click)="onSend()">Send</p-button>
</div>
```

Run the Application

```
ng serve
```

Go to `http://localhost:4200/enhance-cv,`
upload your resume and follow the instructions to
improve your resume.

Congratulations! We have completed our CV enhancer
application.

Code Samples

Visit `https://books.abdelfattah-ragab.com` **to**
download the code samples.

Ionic Application

I created this with Angular for the web, but you can
easily create it for mobile devices.
Just create the Ionic application with Ionic controls and
use the same services and endpoints.
Deploy it to your store, and wow, you can create
amazing apps.

Good luck!

Conclusion

Congratulations! You have read the book "Angular Generative AI: Building an intelligent CV enhancer with Google Gemini". Now you are able to handle all Generative AI scenarios with ease. Remember that learning Angular is an ongoing process. Practice makes perfect — create your own projects, experiment with the features you have learned, and delve into the extensive online resources.

Thank you for joining me in my exploration of Angular. I wish you the best of luck on your programming journey. Have fun programming and good luck with your applications!

Media Attributions

Profile data concept illustration
Image by storyset on Freepik

Modern annual report magazine page flyer a company
catalog
Image by starline on Freepik

Don't miss out!

Receive an email when Abdelfattah Ragab publishes a new book. It's free and without obligation.

Also by Abdelfattah Ragab

Stripe Integration in Angular

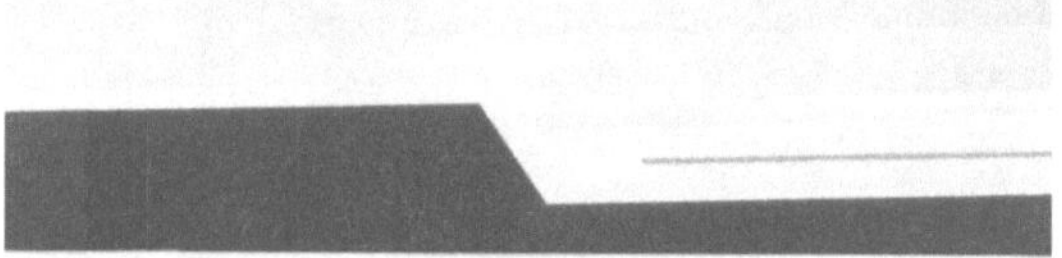

Shippo is a multi-carrier shipping solution designed to streamline the shipping process for businesses of all sizes.
By integrating shipping into your application, you can create better types of e-commerce applications.

You will learn how to create the labels, calculate shipping costs, and get the fastest, cheapest, and best rates.
By the end of the book, you will be able to enable shipping in your Angular application and handle all kinds of scenarios.

Stripe Integration in Angular

Stripe Integration in Angular

A Step-by-Step Guide to Creating
Payment Functionality

Abdelfattah Ragab

Stripe is a leading payment processing platform that
enables businesses to accept online payments.
By integrating payment processing into your application,
you can create all kinds of e-commerce applications.
You will learn how to create the checkout session, how
to use webhooks events and finally how to go live.
By the end of the book, you will be able to process
payments in your Angular application and handle all
kinds of scenarios.

Responsive Layouts: Flex, Grid and Multi-Column

Welcome to the book "Responsive Layouts: Flex, Grid and Multi-Column"
In this book I explain the three best-known responsive layouts: the Flexbox, the Grid and the Multi-Column layout.
Flexbox is a one-dimensional layout that only works in one dimension at a time, either horizontally or vertically.

The grid layout is a two-dimensional layout that distributes the elements horizontally and vertically at the same time.
The multi-column layout is a special layout for magazines and newspapers, where the text should flow in columns with spacing, rules, etc.
I'll explain all the properties and their values and how they affect the distribution of elements on the screen.
So let's get started.

Responsive Design

Responsive design is an approach to web design that ensures web pages render well on a variety of devices and screen sizes, from desktop monitors to mobile phones. The primary goal of responsive design is to provide an optimal viewing experience, making it easy for users to read and navigate the site with minimal resizing, panning, and scrolling.

RESPONSIVE
DESIGN

Angular HTTP

In this book, I explain everything you need to know about connecting to backend Rest APIs from your Angular application.
In this book, I will show you how to invoke different methods like GET, POST, and the like, how to use interceptors to inject an authentication token into every outgoing request, and much more.
We will cover all areas of calling Rest APIs with Angular.

By the end of this book, you will be able to call Rest APIs from your Angular application in any scenario. Let us get started.

Angular Shopping Store

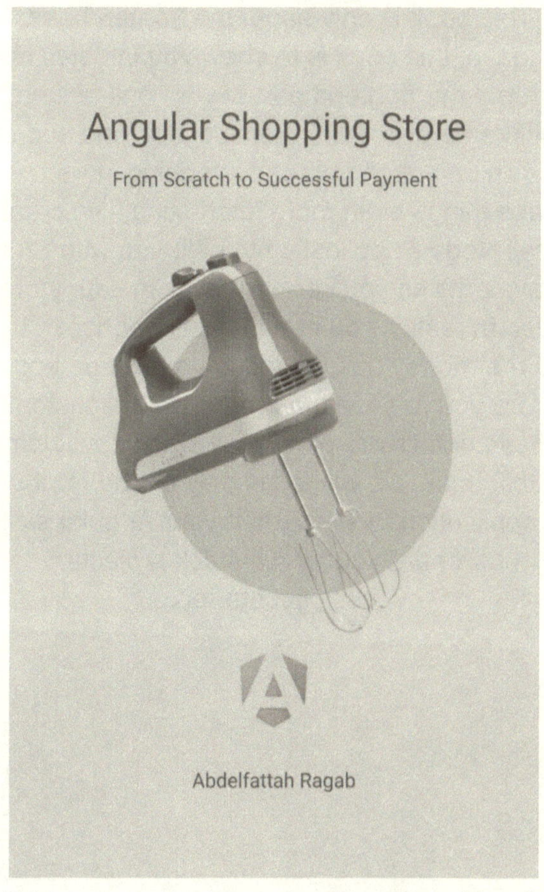

Welcome to the "Angular Shopping Store".

In this book, you'll learn how to create an online
shopping store using the Angular framework.
To get your store up and running, you need more than
Angular.
You need a backend, a database, payment and shipping
gateways and much more.
This book is only about the frontend part.
The goal of this book is to show you in detail how to
create the frontend part of your online store.
You will create everything from scratch and end up with
a complete frontend shopping store.
To make things even more interesting, I've created a
small Nodejs application to help you with Stripe
payments so you can sell items in your store.
However, in reality, you need to use webhooks to make
sure the money has landed in your Stripe account
before you release the product to the customer.
All these details are part of full-stack development.
Also in this book, we will focus only on the front-end part
of the application to strengthen your Angular skills and
prepare you for full-stack projects.
Let's get started.

Shrova Mall

Once you are familiar with Angular, I recommend reading the book "**Shrova Mall**". This is a complete e-commerce solution that allows you to ship products to customers and accept payments online, among other things.

About the Author

Abdelfattah Ragab is a professional software developer with more than 20 years of experience. https://abdelfattah-ragab.com

About the Publisher

Abdelfattah Ragab is a highly qualified and experienced software developer with over 20 years of experience in the industry. Specializing in front-end development, Abdelfattah Ragab has a deep understanding of Angular, JavaScript, TypeScript, HTML and CSS. Read more at https://abdelfattah-ragab.com

www.ingramcontent.com/pod-product-compliance
Lightning Source LLC
LaVergne TN
LVHW041804190726
843493LV00008B/2789